Instruments of the Orchestra

John Hosier   with a Preface by Yehudi Menuhin

Oxford University Press   Music Department
Walton Street, Oxford OX2 6DP

© *Oxford University Press* 1961

New Material © *Oxford University Press 1977*

First published in 1961

Second Edition 1977

Reprinted 1977, 1978, 1980, 1981, 1983, 1985, 1986, 1988, 1989, 1990
ISBN 0 19 321351 6

Printed in Hong Kong

 A cassette containing nearly 100 musical extracts illustrating 35 different instruments is available and may be bought separately (**ISBN 0 19 321353 2**) or in a boxed set with the book (**ISBN 0 19 321352 4**)

Contents

	Preface	6
	Introduction	7
1	About Sound	9
2	The Strings	17
3	The Woodwind	30
4	The Brass	43
5	Percussion	59
6	How the Orchestra Grew	65

Preface

In our days, when we are all endlessly curious and eager to learn how things work, *Instruments of the Orchestra* should help satisfy these basic urges.

I hope this book and the cassette will serve to map the landmarks of sound as clearly in our minds as we visualize the primary colours and the smells of fresh hay, flowers, or Stilton cheese.

In fact, it is a fascinating game to compare particular qualities of sounds with particular tastes, smells or colours as with particular shapes and textures.

I wonder if we would all agree about which sounds were scornful or vengeful, which were kind and which proud or pompous, which flattering and which pure or exalted.

But, in the end, music will be best loved and understood through itself, for itself and by itself – for we *are* music as much as we are anything else.

It has been a delightful experience for me in this enterprise to approach the actual function of each particular instrument, as one never has the opportunity to do at a performance.

Yehudi Menuhin

Introduction

This little book sets out to do no more than describe the main instruments of the orchestra and the principles on which they work. To understand these principles, some knowledge of the nature of sound is necessary, and in the first part of the book I have tried to present the 'scientific' background as simply as possible.

Of course, there is no musical value in learning about single reeds and the length of tubing in a horn unless you can tell the *sound* of a clarinet from the *sound* of a horn, or, indeed, unless you are prepared to enjoy the music they play. So that the reader can relate the appearance and the mechanics of an instrument to its actual sound, this book has been prepared in conjunction with a cassette of musical extracts illustrating all the instruments of the orchestra. Each instrument is introduced by Mr Yehudi Menuhin and its range and tone quality demonstrated by well-known players. As well as short unaccompanied pieces for solo instruments, there are also many extracts from orchestral records, so that solo instruments can be heard in their orchestral setting. The tunes printed in this book are among those played on the cassette. The bars have been numbered so that in classwork teachers can help pupils follow the tunes with the cassette playing, by counting the bars.

I have kept technical musical terms down to a minimum. This has not always been easy. It is rather like talking about football and always having to say 'the man who plays in the middle of the second row' instead of 'the centre half'. There is no mention of transposition: all the tunes (apart from the *Leonora* trumpet call) are written as they sound. Nor have the instruments been related to the full score. In fact, both on the cassette and in the book, the instruments within the four families have been grouped according to their construction rather than to the order in which they appear in a score. Thus, in the section on woodwind, flutes and piccolo are followed by the single-reed instruments, and then come the double-reed instruments, instead of the usual order: piccolo, flute, oboe, cor anglais, clarinet, bass clarinet, bassoon, and double bassoon.

Introduction

Although this book is intended for young people and others exploring the orchestra for the first time, I hope it may be useful to hardened listeners who are a bit vague about how instruments work. A pianist I know, for instance, thinks that a trumpeter automatically gets the right note by pressing down an appropriate valve. This does not matter, I suppose, except that the trumpeter's skill is then very much underestimated; and that is a pity, considering the time it takes him to acquire it.

Since this book first appeared in 1961 there have been considerable changes in the brass department of the orchestra. I would like to acknowledge the help of John Edney and Michael Hinton in bringing the chapter on brass up to date.
    I would also like to express my thanks to Alan Cave for suggesting revisions to the chapter on woodwind. Thanks are due, too, to the photographer, Keith Hawkins, and to the members of the ILEA London Schools Symphony Orchestra who appear in the illustrations, and to Selmer's for the photograph on p. 58.

J.H.

1 About Sound

Thousands of years ago, man found that he could make a sound by blowing across a hole in a hollow bone. Or he could produce a note or two on an animal's horn, by cutting a hole in the side of it, putting his tightened lips against the hole, and blowing through them. A tree trunk, hollowed out and laid on its side, would make a powerful sound when it was beaten with sticks. He could get a faint note by plucking a strip of bark stretched between the ends of a curved stick.

It seems a long way from the hollow bone to the gleaming silver flute, but the principle behind the way they produce their sound is the same. And so it is with the animal's horn and the trumpet, the tree trunk and the timpani, and the stretched strip of bark and the violin. Indeed, between them, the instruments of a modern orchestra seem to represent nearly all the ways in which men have ever made sound.

To make a sound you must first make a vibration. *All sound is caused by vibration:* your voice, your feet on the pavement, the wind in the telegraph wire, the loudspeaker in the wireless set. You can sometimes see and feel the vibrations of sound: touch your throat as you speak; look at a thick string at the bottom of the piano when you press its key; feel the tissue paper tickle your lips when you play a comb and paper.

If you stretch a piece of elastic and then pluck it, you can see the elastic moving very quickly, backwards and forwards. This backward and forward motion causes the particles in the air next to the elastic to move backwards and forwards too, and these particles in turn make the ones next to them move in a similar way. This vibration does not make the air move like a gust of wind. It is passed along rather in the same way that a jolt received at one end of a goods train standing still will be passed along the whole length of the train, one truck touching the next and returning to its original position. But to go back to our elastic band, when the tiny disturbances that the vibrations cause make their way from air particle to air particle, and reach the ear, they act on the sensitive membrane of the ear drum, making it vibrate too, and the brain interprets the vibrations as sound.

Anything that vibrates regularly produces a note – musical sound. Irregular vibrations cause noise. But it is difficult to make hard and fast rules about 'noise' and 'music'. As we saw, the existence of sound, as distinct from vibrations, depends on the ear and the brain. To a deaf person, birds are dumb. To somebody trying to read a book, the regular vibrations of the person next door practising the trumpet may sound like noise. To a hungry person, the irregular vibrations of the clink of dishes being put on the table can sound like music.

A piece of elastic vibrates regularly – so it produces a note. If it makes that backwards and forwards movement 261 times a second it sounds the note middle C. Anything vibrating 261 times a second produces middle C; from a bluebottle's wings to a violin string.

If our elastic vibrates more quickly, that is, if there are more vibrations a second, it produces a higher note: 522 vibrations a second produce the C above middle C; 1,044 vibrations, the C two octaves above middle C. Fewer vibrations produce lower notes: 130 vibrations a second give us the octave below middle C; 65 vibrations the C two octaves below. The high-ness or low-ness of notes is called *pitch*. *Pitch depends on the number of vibrations a second.*

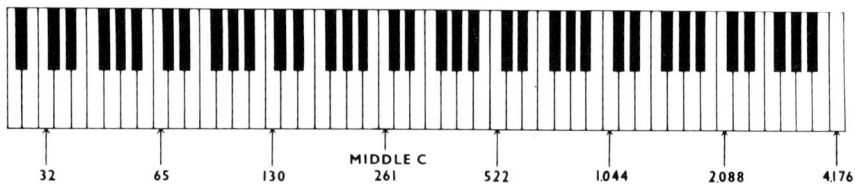

These vibrations per second are approximate.
(Middle C is in fact 261·6 vibrations per second.)

The human ear at its best can hear vibrations between about 20,000 times a second down to about 20 times a second. Children can often hear higher notes than adults. Dogs can hear higher notes than children. On the piano, the bottom A string vibrates about $27\frac{1}{2}$ times a second. The top A vibrates 3,520 times a second. If you compare the strings for top A and bottom A you can see what is needed for high and low notes. The top string is short, tightly stretched and thin – so thin that it needs three strings to give a strong enough note. The bottom string is much longer, not so tightly stretched, and thicker.

In all instruments that produce sounds from vibrating strings – the violin family, guitars, the harp, the piano and so on, the pitch of the notes depends on these three things:
1. The length of the string
2. The *tension* (the tightness) of the string
3. The thickness

(If it were not necessary to consider the size of the instrument, the thickness of strings would not be so important. For instance, if the bottom strings of the piano were as thin as the top ones, then they would have to be nine metres long to produce the right low notes.)

The connection between size and pitch is very important. We have seen that a long string vibrates more slowly than a short string, because there is a great deal more of it to move backwards and forwards. When we come to instruments other than those with strings, size is still important. In woodwind instruments, the air inside the tube of the instrument is made to vibrate. This air enclosed in the tube of the instrument is called a 'column' of air. A long column of air vibrates more slowly than a short column of air. So long wind instruments produce low notes, and short wind instruments produce high notes. *The shorter the vibrating column of air, the higher the note.*

The loudness and softness of notes depends on the *strength* of the vibrations. A length of string, kept stretched at the same tension and given first a gentle tweak and then a violent one, will produce a note of the same pitch each time, but of a different loudness.

In all instruments, the part that vibrates would not produce enough sound, or a particularly pleasing sound, on its own. The vibrating strings of a violin, without the body of the violin, would produce a very feeble sound. It is the body of the violin that magnifies the sound from the strings and gives it its beauty. Because the strings are in contact with the body of the violin, it is made to vibrate too, and so the sound is increased, is given resonance. The body of the violin acts as a *resonator*.

In the piano, the resonator is the wooden sounding board over which the strings are stretched. In the voice, the vocal cords vibrate, and spaces in the mouth and nose give the vibrations resonance.

In the woodwind and brass instruments, the column of air gives resonance to the original vibration. Some resonators (like the body of the violin) vibrate because they are attached to the original vibration. But often a resonator vibrates when it is not even touching the cause of the vibration, because it is in sympathy with the note the vibration is producing.

A rattle in a car will sometimes start when the car reaches a certain speed, because the vibration of the wheels on the road reach a certain pitch, and the rattle responds to that pitch. A singer can sing certain notes that can make a glass vibrate in sympathy. If he does it violently enough, he can break the glass. Or you may have noticed people trying their voices in a small room, like a bathroom. When their voice is at a certain pitch, it seems to 'boom'; this is because the voice has found the 'sympathetic resonance' of a room.

Besides having a fixed resonance, the body of an instrument has parts in it that vibrate in sympathy with certain notes that the instrument is playing.

Now suppose we have five instruments – a piano, a violin, an oboe, a flute, and a trumpet. If the piano and the violin strings are vibrating 440 times a second, and the columns of air in the flute, oboe, and trumpet are vibrating 440 times a second, each of these five instruments is producing the same note, in this case 'A'. Why is it that each note, although it is at the same pitch, sounds different?

First of all, although we say we hear the single note A, we are in fact

About Sound

hearing a mixture of sounds; most instruments never produce a 'pure' note. A string, for example, vibrates along the whole of its free length. But at the same time it vibrates in two halves, in three thirds, and so on. Each of these other vibrations gives off a higher sound.

The whole length vibrates, and so do the two halves, and the three thirds

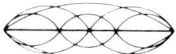

Several sections are therefore vibrating at the same time

The note of the whole length of string vibrating is the one that we pick out most strongly; but the other sections of the string that are vibrating give off faint notes too. These are called *overtones*.

When you play the note G on the piano, in the bottom line of the bass stave, the following overtones reach our ears:

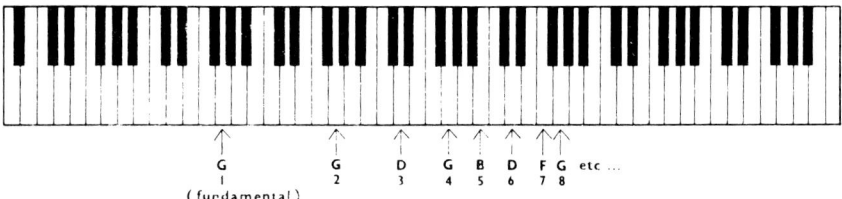

To sort them out more clearly, press down as many of the notes on the piano as you can manage that correspond with these overtones, starting with 2, *without making them sound*. Put your foot on the sustaining pedal, strike bottom G (note 1) sharply, and take off the sustaining pedal immediately. You will be able to distinguish one or two of the overtones very clearly. Because your fingers are pressed down on the keys, the strings of the upper notes are free to vibrate in sympathy with the overtones produced by bottom G.

Here are the first sixteen overtones that it is possible to get from one note (the black notes sound out of tune):

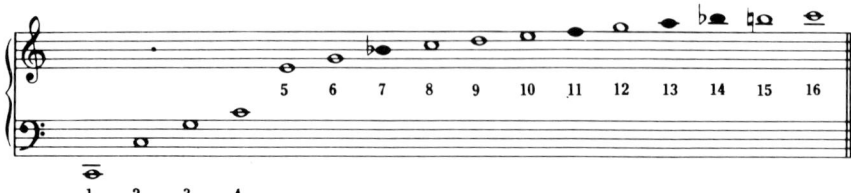

You can see that the gaps between the notes get smaller as they get higher, and after 16 they are even closer together. The overtones change according to the bottom note (the *fundamental*), but the gaps between them are always in the same proportion. If the fundamental is G, the overtones 2, 4, 8, and 16 will be Gs. If the fundamental is C, then the overtones 2, 4, 8, and 16 will be Cs. And so on.

Some instruments produce more overtones than others; and different instruments emphasize different overtones. Occasionally you can hear an almost pure note, without overtones: the recorder, for instance, or low notes played softly on a flute; and a tuning fork will give you a quite pure note.

The mixture of overtones gives us the tone colour of the instrument. Instruments that produce notes with a lot of high overtones sound bright; low overtones make an instrument sound mellow.

Different instruments produce different mixtures of overtones because of the ways the instruments are built; their method of producing vibrations; the materials of which they are made; the kind of resonators they have. And as we saw earlier on, the body of an instrument has parts in it that vibrate in sympathy with certain notes, and these parts have

About Sound   15

This is note A as it sounds on the flute and the oboe. The length of the black line shows the strength of the overtones.

The overtones produced by a flute playing 'A'

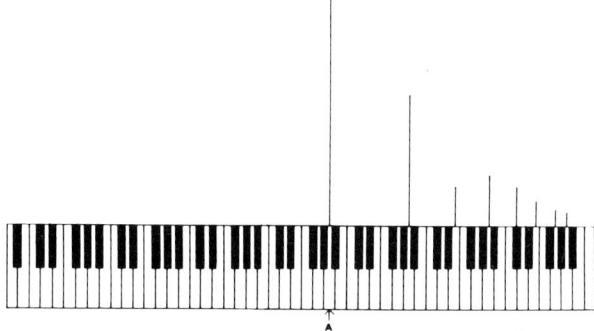

The overtones produced by an oboe playing 'A'

Although we hear this note as 'A', some of the overtones, strangely enough, are stronger than the fundamental note.

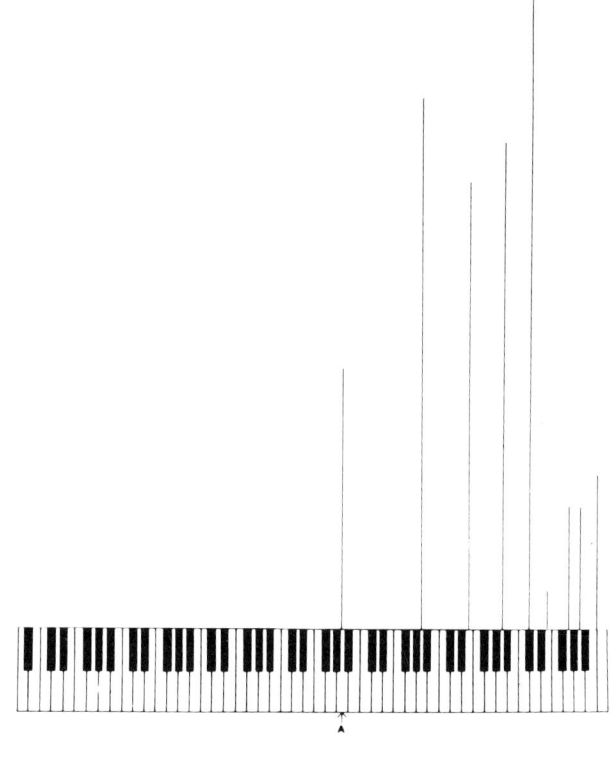

their overtones too. It is obvious but true to say that reed instruments produce reedy sounds. Brass instruments produce brassy sounds. In the next part of the book we shall look at the instruments much more closely.

The important things to remember from this chapter are:
1. You need a vibration to produce sound
2. The shorter the string or the vibrating column of air, the quicker the vibrations
3. The quicker the vibrations, the higher the sound
4. A resonator gives body and character to the original vibrations
5. A particular blend of overtones gives the quality, or the tone colour, of each instrument.

2 The Strings

The violin family (the violin, the viola, the violoncello – or *cello* for short – and the double bass) makes up the string section of the orchestra. Although the harp is strictly speaking a string instrument, it is usually considered on its own.

More than half the modern orchestra is made up of strings, and you will often find sixteen first violins, fourteen second violins, twelve violas, ten cellos, and eight double basses.

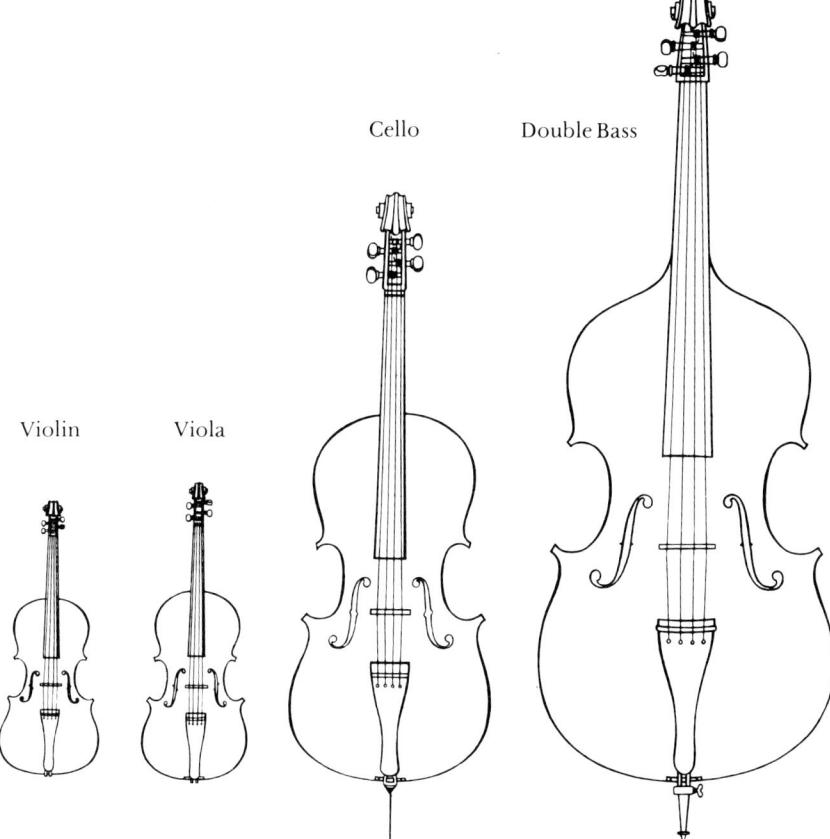

The Strings

Violin

Range:

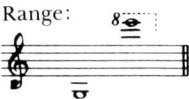

The four strings are tuned to these notes:

First and second *violins* are the same instruments, of course; it is just that violins in the orchestra are divided into two groups, all the violins in the first group playing one part, and all the violins in the second group playing another part.

The violin is the smallest member of the orchestral strings, and plays the highest notes. It has four strings stretched across a hollow wooden box. The strings are generally made of steel, nylon, or gut with a covering of fine metal wire, usually aluminium. Some players still prefer plain gut strings. The top side of the box is usually made of pine and the rest of sycamore wood. The strings are fixed at one end to the tail piece and to the tuning pegs at the other.

The G string is the thickest, and the E, naturally, the thinnest. The tuning pegs enable the player to put the strings at the right tension to sound the four 'open' notes, in other words, to 'tune' the strings.

The strings are kept from touching the body of the instrument by the raised bridge over which they are stretched. The bridge also conducts the vibrations from the strings to the box.

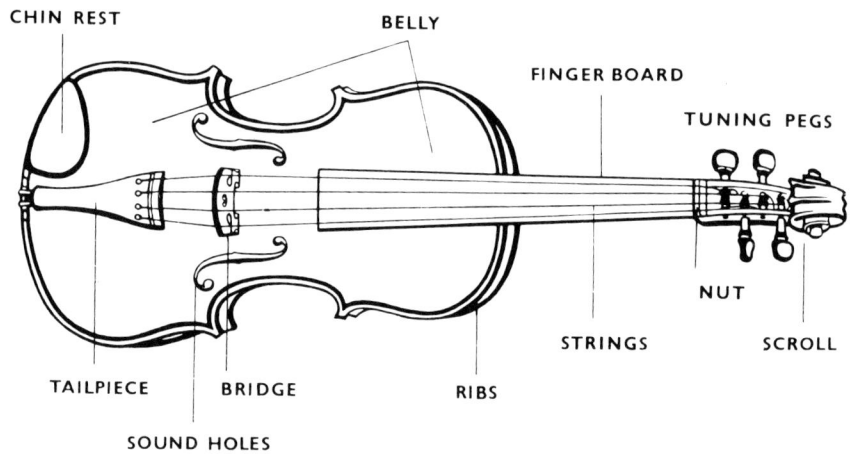

The Strings

To produce a sound, the player must first make the strings vibrate. He usually does this with a bow. The bow is a wooden stick along which hair from a horse's tail is stretched. From a distance, the hair on a bow looks like a flat strip of ribbon; but when the bow is slackened, you can see that it is in fact made up of a great many hairs. The bow is made sticky with 'resin' (usually pronounced 'rosin') and as it is drawn across a string of the violin, it keeps on catching the string and pulling it. Of course, as the string is tightly stretched, it will only allow the bow to pull it so far and then it springs back. The stickiness of the bow then catches the string again, and so the process is repeated. This constant pulling and letting go of the string causes it to vibrate and then we get a note.

To get different notes, the player changes the length of the strings (as we saw, the shorter the string, the higher the note). He does this by pressing the string with his finger against the finger board, 'stopping' the string. The string, instead of vibrating all the way from the bridge to the end of the finger board (the 'nut'), only vibrates from the bridge to the player's finger.

There are no marked positions where the player puts his finger to produce different notes; he is guided by his ear.

When the string vibrates, the vibrations are then taken by the bridge through to the belly of the violin, which vibrates too. Inside the body of the violin, a sound post takes the vibrations from the belly to the back of the violin at the same time making the air inside the body vibrate. The body of the violin, vibrating with the strings, magnifies the sound of the strings and gives it much greater beauty.

Although the violin is only about 60cm long, nearly eighty separate pieces, all carefully fitted together, go to make it up. The finest violins were made in the late sixteenth and seventeenth centuries in Italy, by the Stradivari, Guarneri, and Amati families.

The violin has changed hardly at all during the last 350 years or so; it has been made about half an inch longer, the bridge has been made higher, and, at the beginning of the nineteenth century, the chin rest

The Strings

was added. All other instruments in the orchestra, apart from the strings, have undergone enormous changes during the years – and where a violinist would rush to get hold of a Stradivarius violin, a flautist would find a modern flute much more satisfactory.

The violin is the most flexible of all instruments. Like the voice it has a tremendous range of expression. The player has exact control over the bow, and by making changes in the way he applies the bow to the string, he can alter the sound he gets. He can play very quietly or very loudly, he can start quietly and get louder, or vice versa. He can go from one note to another smoothly; or he can detach each note and make it sound quite separate.

Here are some names for special ways of using the bow:

Spiccato: making each note short and crisp.

Saltallato (or saltando, saltato): these words describe the action of making the bow bounce up and down on the strings (saltando is Italian for 'leaping'). The string vibrates every time the bow bounces on it, in tiny bursts. The effect is crisp and light.

Martellato (Italian for 'hammered'): making each note strongly and separately.

For special effects the player can use the wooden part of the bow – the 'stick' – instead of the horse hair. He then plays *col legno* (Italian for 'with the wood'). In this case he does not draw the bow over the strings, but 'taps' them.

Another very special effect is *sul ponticello* ('on the bridge') where the player has to bow the string on or near the bridge instead of about halfway between the bridge and the finger board as he usually does. *Sul ponticello* makes a weak, eerie sound.

By making the bow quiver very rapidly, the player gets a shivering effect called *tremolo* (like 'tremble').

Tremolo is not the same as *vibrato*. You will notice all string players 'shaking' the left hand as it stops the strings when they are not playing very quickly. This makes every note wobble a tiny bit in and out of tune.

Violins and violas

This vibrato makes string tone warmer and richer, and it is very effective when many string instruments are playing together.

The bow can be made to make two strings vibrate at the same time so that two notes can be played at once. This is called 'double stopping'. 'Triple stopping' means three strings played at the same time. To play four strings, the player must very quickly touch the bottom string before the others.

A mute is a small clip that can be fixed on the bridge of the instrument to deaden some of the vibrations from the strings. The mute makes the instrument sound veiled and muffled. *Con sordino* means 'muted'.

Earlier on we noticed that a string vibrates in several ways at once. As the whole free length of it vibrates, at the same time sections of it vibrate too – the two halves, the three thirds, the four quarters, and so on. If you were to place your finger very lightly exactly halfway along the length of a vibrating string, you would stop the whole length vibrating and just allow the two halves to vibrate. Then we hear the note an octave higher than the note of the full string. It sounds weak and ghostly. This note is called a *harmonic*. By lightly touching the string a third of the way along its length, you get a harmonic sounding twelve notes higher. And by using two fingers there are ways of producing other harmonics too.

So far, we have assumed that the player is producing his sounds with a bow. But he can also put his bow aside and pluck the strings with his fingers. This is called *pizzicato*.

All the above effects can also be obtained from the other instruments of the violin family: the viola, the cello, and the double bass.

Viola

Range:

The four strings are tuned to these notes:

C G D A

The *viola* is slightly larger than the violin, and is held in the same way. The strings are thicker and, of course, longer; and the bow, although the same length as the violin bow, is heavier.

The viola is the tenor of the violin family. It does not have the sparkling, brilliant sound of the violin. Its tone is warm and dark. The slightly tart flavour of the sound in the upper ranges of the D and A strings is unique to the viola.

The viola was for many years the Cinderella of the orchestra – filling in dull parts in the middle of the music, or sometimes copying the cellos when they had a tune. Since Berlioz (1803–69), however, composers have given much more interesting music to the violas.

Mozart: Sinfonia Concertante, K. 364

Violoncello (cello)

Range:

The four strings are tuned to these notes:

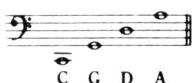

C G D A

The *violoncello* is usually called simply the *cello*. The cello is too big to tuck under the chin, of course. Originally it was gripped between the knees of the player. During the last century a spike was added to the bottom of the instrument and nowadays this spike supports the instrument.

The cello has longer, thicker strings than the viola, and therefore plays lower notes.

Once upon a time the cellos did little else but play the bass line to support the rest of the string family. But the instrument has a glorious singing tenor range as well. During the last 150 years or so, composers have been giving cellos too their share of the tunes.

Double bass

Range:

The four strings are tuned to these notes:

The violin, the viola, and the cello have a similar shape; the difference is in their size. The *double bass,* the biggest member of the string family, has a slightly different shape from the others. It has sloping shoulders, for example, and its back is flat and not curved. In fact, the double bass probably came to the violin group from the viol family. Viols and violins existed side by side in the sixteenth and seventeenth centuries. Viols were very popular in private music making. They had a sweeter and more subdued tone than the violin. However, with music being used more and more as public entertainment, the powerful violin family took the lead. There are nowadays four strings on the double bass (and very thick they are too), although occasionally you see five. The bow is shorter than those of the other string instruments.

Double bass solos are very rare. The double basses usually play the bass part of an octave below the cellos; but since the end of the last

Cellos and double basses

century, composers have often given the double basses a separate part of their own. The pizzicato on the double bass is a splendidly strong and vibrant sound.

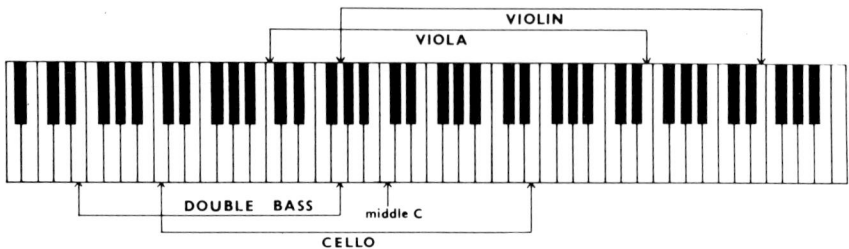

The range of string instruments
(The top notes shown here are approximate)

Harp

The *harp* is a plucked string instrument, so it comes between the string family and the percussion family. It is one of the oldest of all instruments, but it is only within the last 150 years that it has become a regular member of the orchestra.

    The harpist does not have to 'stop' his strings as the violin player does. The harp strings are already 'cut to size', the long ones for the low notes, and the short ones for the high notes. The different sizes of string account for the triangular shape of the harp – the short strings nearest the player and the longest further away. The strings vary in thickness; the thickest are the low notes. Some strings are made of gut and some of metal. Although the strings are of the right length and the right thickness, the player still has to put them at the right tension. He (or very often she) does this by turning the pegs to which the strings are attached. The harpist is usually the first instrumentalist to arrive on the concert platform to tune each one of his strings before the concert starts.

The Strings

Harp

The Strings

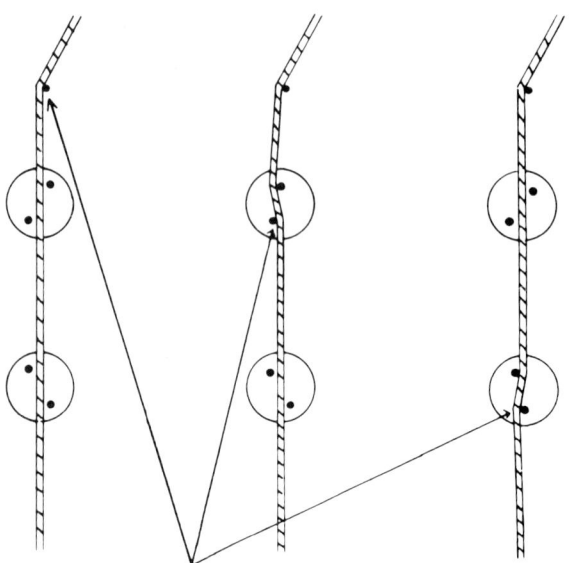

STOPPING MECHANISM: STRING VIBRATES BELOW HERE

| The pedal is up, and the string left to vibrate. | When the pedal is pressed down one notch the discs turn, bringing the studs of the top disc against the string, thus 'stopping' it and making it shorter. | The pedal is pressed down two notches, bringing the studs of the lower disc against the string and making it shorter still. |

There are usually forty-seven strings on the harp; some of them are coloured so that they stand out and the harpist knows where he is. Forty-seven strings do not give enough different notes for most music, so each string can be made to give three different notes. This is where the pedals come in. Although the harpist seems to do all the work with the tips of his fingers, his feet are kept busy all the time too. The harp has seven pedals, one for all the *dohs,* one for all the *rays,* and so on. If the player presses the pedal for *doh* down a notch, a metal stud is pushed against the ends of all the *doh* strings making them a little shorter and sound a little higher (a semitone). If he pushes the pedal down two notches then another stud shortens the strings even more, making the string sound higher again (a tone). Thus when the pedal which controls all the C strings is in the 'up' position, all these strings sound C flats. When the pedal is depressed one notch, they sound C naturals. Two notches, and they sound C sharps. The other pedals make the other strings work in the same way: flat, natural, sharp. Thus when all the pedals are up, the harp plays in the key of C flat major. The player is adjusting his pedals all the time to give him the right selection of notes.

The mechanism that alters the notes goes from the pedals, up the inside of the elaborately decorated column of the harp. The thick bottom part of the frame, the sounding-board, is a resonator (like the body of the violin).

Besides playing tunes, the harpist can set the notes of a chord and play them very quickly one after the other over the whole range of the instrument. Chords spread out in this way are called *arpeggios* from the Italian name for the harp, *arpa.*

The harpist is often asked to play a *glissando* – and this means he sweeps his fingers over the strings.

Like the violinist he can play *harmonics:* at the same time as he plucks the string he lightly touches it halfway along its length with the side of his hand. The note he produces then has a bell-like quality, sounding an octave higher than the note produced by the 'open' string.

Sometimes the harpist is asked to stop the string vibrating almost as soon as he has plucked it, producing a dry sound very unlike the usual full, warm one. This effect is known by the French term *sons étouffés* (smothered sounds). Another French term *sons près de la table* (sounds near the sounding-board) describes the guitar-like sound the harpist gets by plucking the string near the sounding-board.

3 The Woodwind

In the orchestra you usually find two flutes (and very often a piccolo); two oboes (and sometimes a cor anglais); two clarinets (and sometimes a bass clarinet); two bassoons (and sometimes a double bassoon).

Wood and wind each have their contribution to make to woodwind instruments. The instruments are tubes generally made of wood (although metal is very often used for flutes and piccolos, and oboes and clarinets are occasionally made of ebonite – rubber hardened by the addition of sulphur). The wind is the player's breath which is used to make the air in the tube vibrate. Wind is rather a misleading word. Simply blowing down a tube does not make the sound. A vibration must be set up first. The player does this with his breath, in different ways according to his particular instrument.

Once the air in the tube is set vibrating, it produces a note according to its length. Long columns of air produce low notes, short columns, high notes.

You can see this very simply in the panpipes: tubes of different length, put side by side.

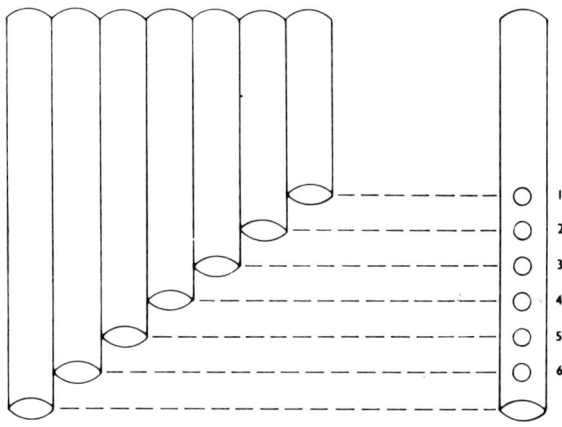

The Woodwind

But you can also get different lengths of vibrating air from one pipe by opening and shutting holes cut in the side. The air vibrates only between the mouth end of the tube (where the vibration is started) and the nearest uncovered hole. If we take a pipe with six holes and close all the holes the air will vibrate for the whole length of the pipe and we get the lowest note of the pipe. If we open the sixth hole, then the air in the tube will vibrate only as far as that hole. We get a slightly shorter tube and a slightly higher note. And so on.

We saw that a string vibrates in several ways at once. If you lightly touch the string, you can stop the whole length vibrating and get the sound produced by half its length vibrating – and this sound is eight notes (an octave) higher.

In woodwind instruments you produce notes an octave higher by 'overblowing'. (The clarinet family produces a note a twelfth higher.) In the flute, the player speeds up the vibrations, making them too quick for the whole tube to respond to. In the oboe and clarinet, a small hole is opened which lets air in at a special place to stop the whole length of the column of air vibrating. This is rather like the violinist gently touching the string. With these methods the range of the instruments is increased considerably.

Now, if you take a pipe with six holes in it, close all the holes, and make the air vibrate inside the pipe, you have *doh*. Open the hole nearest the end, the sixth, you have *ray*; fifth hole, *me*; fourth hole, *fah*; third hole, *soh*; second hole, *lah*; first hole, *te*; and if you close all the holes, make the air vibrate quicker – overblow – you get top *doh,* an octave higher than your bottom *doh*. And all woodwind instruments, no matter how complicated they look, are built from these principles. The clarinet overblowing produces a sound twelve notes higher (e.g. *doh-soh'*), because in its case the tube is 'stopped' (see p 35).

Nowadays the notes between the eight notes of the scale (like the black notes in the scale of C on the piano) are produced by extra holes; and small vent holes are used to allow the player to 'overblow' – play in higher octaves. Also, holes that are convenient for the players do not always produce notes that are in tune. The modern key mechanism has been developed so that he can cover and uncover holes to which his fingers would not stretch, by remote control. And that is why modern woodwind instruments are covered with such an elaborate arrangement of metal keys and levers.

We have mentioned breath and fingers. The player's tongue is also important. With it he can give every note a clear start; and by *not* using it, he can go smoothly from note to note.

When we refer to the flute nowadays we mean the flute that is held sideways (the transverse flute). The recorder, however, is a member of the flute family, and was used in orchestras in the days of Bach and Handel. In the recorder, the air is conducted along a narrow channel, and split against a sharp edge – this splitting setting up a disturbance in the tube. Whistles work on the same principle.

The stream of air split in a recorder

Flute

Range:

In the transverse *flute,* the player himself directs the stream of air with his lips against the opposite edge of the mouth hole, where the stream of air is split. This sets the column of air in the tube vibrating. (You can do the same sort of thing by blowing across a bottle top.) The 'transverse' flute, which we shall refer to simply as the 'flute' from now on, was more expressive than the recorder; and it is the one that has been used in orchestras for nearly two hundred years.

The flute is a tube about 67cm long, pretty well cylindrical in shape (i.e. the same thickness all the way along). The mouth hole is cut in the side of the flute near one end. This end is sealed with a stopper. The other end of the tube is open.

The low notes of the flute are soft and haunting but they get brighter and more brilliant the higher they go up. The flute is a very agile instrument. And by making his tongue say (very quickly and silently) T-K, T-K, T-K, or T-K-T, T-K-T, T-K-T, the flautist can make a succession of very fast notes sound crisp and clear.

The flautist is sometimes asked to do 'flutter tonguing'; he rolls an R on his breath as he blows across the mouth hole. This effect is rather like a cat purring.

Many modern scores call for a 'bass' flute in G. Its bottom note is G, a fourth below the normal concert flute. This flute is now becoming universally known as the 'alto' flute.

This is convenient because there is another bass flute, which has a range an octave below the concert flute. This bass flute in C is very rare indeed, but can sometimes be seen in recording studios for use in film and television music.

Piccolo

Range:

The *piccolo,* the little flute, can be played by all flautists. The piccolo is constructed like a flute, but it is half the size and therefore plays higher, an octave higher. The piccolo plays the highest notes in the orchestra, and makes a very shrill sound.

Piccolo and flute

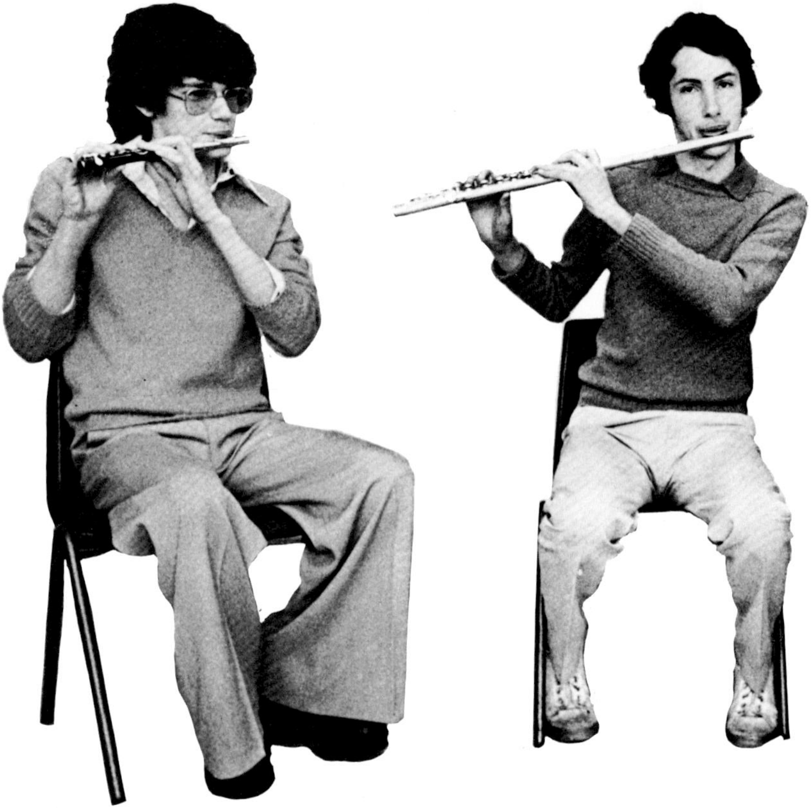

Allegro
Piccolo (sounding an octave higher)
Rossini: Overture to 'Semiramide'
p
p

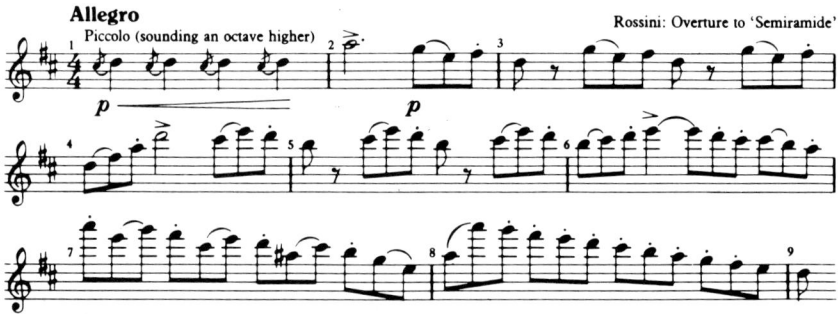

Clarinet

Range:

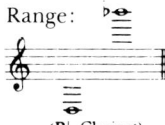

(B♭ Clarinet)

The *clarinet* is about 66cm long, and (like the flute) it is mainly cylindrical. The vibration is made by a reed. This reed is a flat piece of cane, scraped down until, at the end that goes in the player's mouth, it is almost as thin as paper. The reed is fixed over the oblong hole cut in the wedge-shaped mouthpiece. When the player forces air into the mouthpiece, he makes the reed vibrate, and the vibrating reed sets up a vibration in the air in the tube.

The mouthpiece of the flute is open to the air when the flautist is playing. When the clarinettist is playing he has the mouthpiece cushioned between his lips, so that the end of the tube is closed. Because it is cylindrical and because it is closed at one end, the clarinet is called a 'stopped' pipe, and it can produce lower notes than an 'open' pipe of a similar length. It has a very wide range.

The lowest part of the range has a hollow, yet rich sound; the middle part of the range is creamy. High up, the clarinet sounds rather shrill.

It is a very expressive instrument, able to play very quietly, or to get gradually louder and softer. In expressiveness it is rather like the violin, so it is not surprising that it takes the violin parts in military band music.

36 The Woodwind

Bass clarinet and clarinet

The Woodwind

Bass clarinet

Range:

As the *bass clarinet* is twice as long as the ordinary clarinet, it produces notes an octave lower. The bell end is made of metal and is curved upwards. The mouthpiece end is also bent round, so that the player can reach the reed. The bass clarinet looks something like a saxophone, except that the saxophone is all metal. It was the inventor of the saxophone, Adolphe Sax, who made the first good bass clarinet.

Tchaikovsky: Dance of the Sugar Plum Fairy

The small E flat clarinet is a member of the military band and it is occasionally used in the orchestra. It can play higher notes than the ordinary clarinet. The contrabass clarinet is rarely called for in the symphony orchestra (Schoenberg uses it in his Five Orchestral Pieces). It sounds an octave lower than the bass.

Oboe

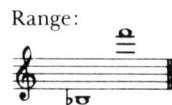

Range:

The *oboe* is a double-reed instrument. The double reed is a narrow strip of cane that is scraped very thin, folded over double, and tied to a fine metal tube. The fold is then cut through, leaving the two pieces of reed fixed closely together. The player puts the doubled reed into his mouth, and by gently forcing his breath between them he makes the reeds vibrate against each other. In this way they start the air in the tube vibrating.

The oboe's tube, which is about 63cm long, is different from the clarinet's. The oboe has a *conical* tube, that is to say, it gets wider towards the bell.

The sound of the oboe is, naturally enough, reedy. It has a rather plaintive quality, and is very good at melancholy tunes. Although it is usually given expressive solos to play, it can be quite lively – and it can sound quite spiteful, too.

Schubert: Symphony No. 9

Cor anglais

Range:

The *cor anglais* is really a large oboe, with a correspondingly lower voice. It has a double reed, and a conical tube. The reed fits on to a curved metal crook about 6cm long; and there is a bulge at the bell end of the instrument. The player often supports the instrument on a sling round his neck. The cor anglais has a very expressive, melancholy voice; and it is always given slowish tunes to play, often in imitation of a shepherd's pipe.

The Woodwind

Cor anglais means 'English horn' – which is rather puzzling as it is neither English, nor a horn. 'Anglais' might come from 'anglé' which means 'bent', referring to the bend in the crook.

Oboe and cor anglais

The Woodwind

[Largo — Cor Anglais, Dvořák: 'New World' Symphony]

Bassoon

Range:

The *bassoon* is another double-reed instrument with a conical bore. It is just over 2.5m long; but it is doubled up on itself, to make the instrument manageable. The 'doubling up' is done in the butt joint of the instrument, which has two parallel pasages bored in it that meet at the bottom. The top end of one passage connects with the crook that leads to the reed; the other connects to the tube that becomes the bell. The double reed, which is much wider than the oboe's, is fixed on to the end of a curved metal tube called the 'crook'. The player supports the instrument with a sling or a spike.

[Allegro moderato — 2 Bassoons, Bizet: 'Dragons D'Alcala' from 'Carmen']

Bassoon and double bassoon

The Woodwind

The bassoon is the bass of the woodwind family. But as you can see from the range, the bassoon has a wide tenor register too. This upper register is often used by composers, and it is particularly good for expressive solos. The lower register is rather dry and gruff; and adds an edge to the lower part of the orchestra.

Double bassoon

Range:

The *double bassoon* is twice as long (5.5m) as the ordinary bassoon, and it sounds an octave lower. It has a conical tube and a double reed. Its very deep voice is used to reinforce the bass, and it is only used with a fairly large orchestra. Surprisingly enough, in spite of its size, the double bassoon is a very flexible instrument. The double bassoon is also known as the contrabassoon.

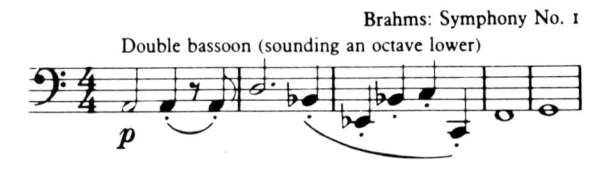

Brahms: Symphony No. 1
Double bassoon (sounding an octave lower)

The range of woodwind instruments
(The top notes shown here are approximate)

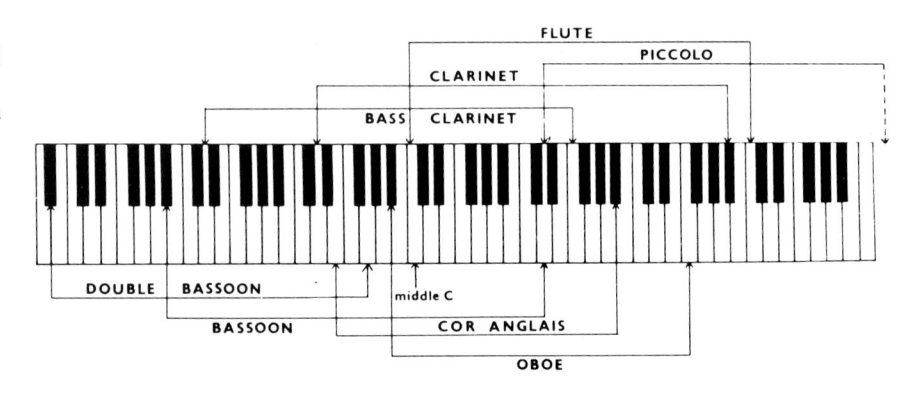

4 The Brass

In an orchestra there are usually four horns (but because continuous playing in certain registers is extremely fatiguing to the horn-player's lips, an additional player, known as a 'bumper', often sits with the horn section, to help out when necessary); two or three trumpets; two tenor trombones; one bass trombone; and one tuba.

Brass instruments are simply brass tubes. The player makes the air in the tube vibrate with his lips. He tenses his lips against a specially shaped mouthpiece, and by blowing through them, he makes them vibrate, rather in the same way that the double reed in an oboe is made to vibrate. The effect is rather like a controlled 'raspberry'. Slack lips vibrate slowly and produce low notes; tight lips vibrate quickly and produce high notes.

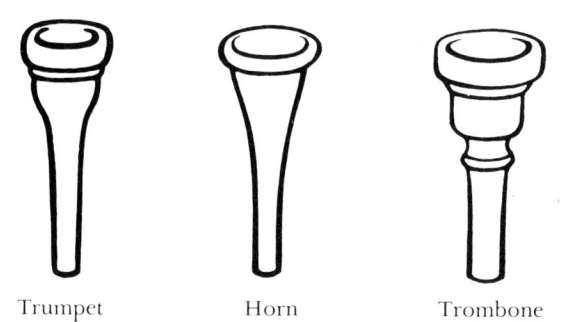

Mouthpieces: Trumpet   Horn   Trombone

Vibrations from his lips against the mouthpiece set the air in the brass tube vibrating. From a length of brass tubing you get a set number of notes – a note for the whole column of air vibrating, a note for half the column, a note for a third of the column, and so on. (The same sort of thing happens with a vibrating string when the violinist plays 'harmonics' and in a woodwind instrument when the player overblows.)

A tube 2.4m long produces all these notes. They make up the 'harmonic series'.

Note 1 (the fundamental note) is usually impossible on tubes of a narrow bore. And the black notes sound out of tune. The player selects any note from this series by putting his lips at the appropriate tension. As you can see, the gaps between the lower notes of the series are wide, and they get closer together as they get higher, until you get a scale between 8 and 16. (The series goes higher than this, but the notes are very difficult to produce.) The fundamental is repeated at 2, 4, 8, 16. A different length of tubing produces a different fundamental, with its corresponding harmonic series.

From a brass tube of 1.2m a player can get these notes easily:

With these notes you can play bugle calls but, because there are gaps between them, it would be impossible to play a simple tune that moves in steps, like 'God save the Queen'.

The Brass

To play just these few bars of music you would need three tubes of different lengths producing three different sets of notes; and you would need to be able to change quickly from one tube to another. The number over each note of the tune shows which of these three sets of notes could provide it.

The valves used in modern brass instruments provide different lengths of tube at the touch of a finger. A valve joins an extra piece of tubing to the instrument, changing the overall length of the tube, and of course changing the harmonic series. Here is a simplified diagram of the trumpet showing how the valves connect the extra lengths of tube.

The dots show the column of air that will vibrate. In 'B' valve 1 has been pressed down to bring in an extra loop of tube. The length of the loop attached to valve 1 produces the difference of a tone; to valve 2, the difference of a semitone; and to valve 3 the difference of $1\frac{1}{2}$ tones. Thus the combined length of the loops attached to valves 1 and 2 is the same as the loop at valve 3.

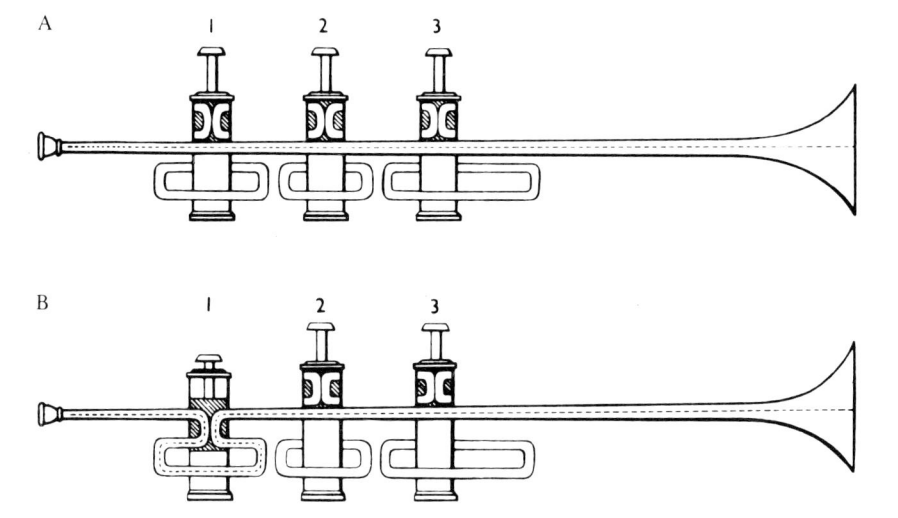

With the original length of the instrument, and the various combinations of three valves, you can get seven different lengths of tube.

On all brass instruments the player does not automatically get the note he wants by pressing the valve, as a pianist does by pressing the key. The valve gives the player the right length of tubing from which he must get the note of the harmonic series he wants by using his lips.

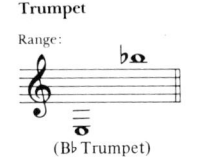

The modern *trumpet* is a more or less cylindrical tube, usually 1.2m long if it has C as its fundamental note, or 1.3m if it has B flat. The player uses a cup-shaped mouthpiece.

In Bach's day, the trumpets were 7 or 8ft long (about 2.4m) with the tube bent round to make it convenient to hold. Just by using his lips (there were no valves) and a shallow mouthpiece, the player could get the high notes of the harmonic series (8–16) and play tunes. By the time of Haydn, Mozart, and Beethoven, the skill of playing these high notes was dying out, and these composers had to make do with the lower notes of the harmonic series. Here is a trumpet call by Beethoven. Compare it with the notes of the harmonic series on page 44.

In those days the trumpet player had separate lengths of metal tubing called 'crooks' which he could fit on to the instrument to change its length, but he could still only play the harmonic series of that length, and it took a little time to make the change. Valves were invented early in the nineteenth century, and the length of the tube could be changed

The Brass

B♭ trumpet, D trumpet, and piccolo trumpet

as quickly as the player wanted. In time the trumpet was shortened to 4½ or 4ft (1.3 or 1.2m).

Because of the demands of the modern recording studio, where absolute accuracy and appropriate tone qualities are essential, the player finds that a certain instrument will give him security in a particular range of notes. The most commonly used trumpets are still the ones built with the fundamental notes of B flat and C, but in addition to these, D and E flat trumpets are sometimes used, as well as the piccolo (small) B flat instrument (sounding an octave higher than the normal B flat trumpet) for very high trumpet parts (in Bach, for example).

The trumpet player may carry as many as four different instruments with him, built in different pitches to suit the range and character of trumpet parts for the wide repertoire of music, from the baroque to the present day, that he is called upon to play. Often, a player may use different instruments within the same piece of music.

Allegro giusto — Tchaikovsky: Fantasy-Overture 'Romeo and Juliet'

Trumpets have a bright, ringing sound. But for special effects, they can be 'muted'. This makes them quieter, and also changes the tone colour. The player puts the mute, which looks like an ice cream cone, in the bell of the instrument. There are several kinds of mute including a 'wow-wow', a 'cup', a 'plunger', and a 'bucket', all frequently used in popular music.

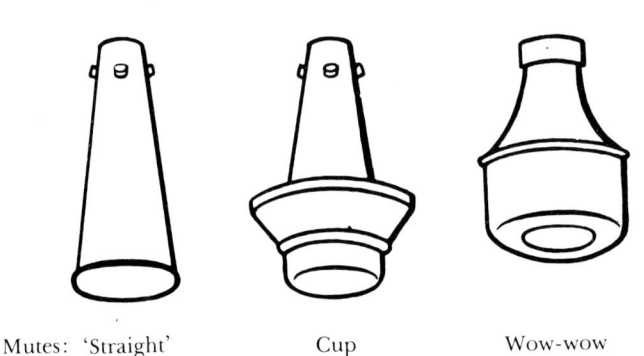

Mutes: 'Straight'   Cup   Wow-wow

Trumpets and cornets

Cornet

The *cornet* is 1.3m long (the same length as a B flat trumpet) and it has valves like the trumpet. The cornet, however, has conical tubing and not cylindrical tubing. It takes a very expert ear to tell the difference between the two instruments. Usually the cornet is played with more vibrato than a trumpet (see violin section for vibrato). The cornet is very flexible and expressive, and is to the brass band what violins are to the orchestra. French composers often ask for cornets as well as trumpets in their music.

Trombone

Tenor trombone range:

Bass trombone range:

Trombones have cylindrical tubing which, apart from one U bend at the end of the slide, is quite straight. It is played with a deep, cup-shaped mouthpiece. Instead of finger valves, the player alters the length of the tube by pushing out a section of the tubing called the slide. The length of the tenor trombone, with the slide in, is about 2.5m. By using his slide, the player can get seven different lengths of tube, each one with its own series of notes which the player gets with his lips. There are no 'notches' to tell the player where each of the positions of the slide is — like the violinist, the trombonist uses his ear as his guide.

The trombone goes back about six hundred years (its old name was the sackbut). Because of its slide mechanism, it has always been able to play all the notes in its range, unlike the old valveless trumpets and horns.

In the middle of the sixteenth century at least four instruments were in use, a soprano, an alto, a tenor and a bass, each corresponding to the range of the equivalent human voice.

In the symphony orchestra, the most common combination of trombone voices has been two tenors and a bass. In the modern orchestra, the first tenor is usually played on a 'single' instrument, pitched in B flat, described above, or on a 'double' instrument. The double instrument has a thumb valve which brings extra tubing into play, which changes the overall length of the instrument and lowers the fundamental note from B flat to (usually) F. Thus all the slide positions on an instrument switched from B flat to F will sound a fourth lower. The player can use either the B flat or the F aspect of the instrument instantaneously to suit the range of the part he is playing. This extra convenience can also reduce some of the slide movements necessary on a single instrument. For example, to play a B flat in the bass clef, followed by a B natural, a difference in pitch of a semitone, on a single instrument will mean a shift from first position (slide right in) to seventh (slide fully extended). With a double instrument the player can produce one of the notes on the B flat side of the instrument, and the other on the

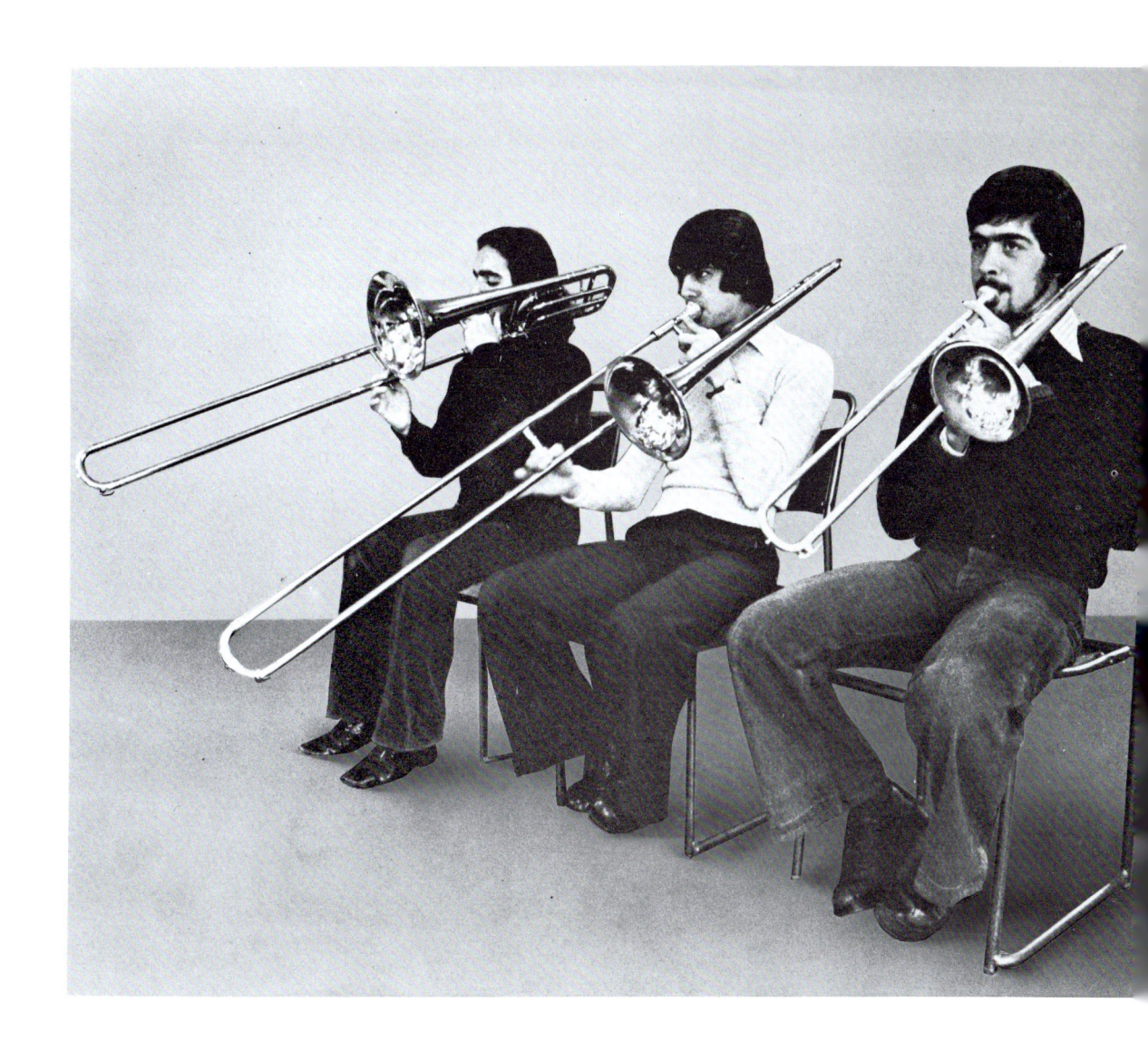

B♭/F bass trombone, B♭ tenor trombone, and E♭ alto trombone

F side, with the use of thumb valve and only a small movement (one position) of the slide.

This double instrument is usually employed by the second player of the three. The bass trombone part is usually played on a double B flat/F instrument with a wider bore, which facilitates the production of good low notes.

An E flat alto trombone (a fourth higher than the tenor) and a double bass trombone (sounding about a fifth lower than the bass) are also used from time to time in symphony and opera orchestras.

The three trombones playing together loudly can sound particularly powerful and awe-inspiring when necessary. But they are also capable of playing quietly.

Trombones can be muted for certain effects. And they are occasionally asked to slide from one note to the next (the player continues to 'blow' and pulls the slide in or out at the same time). This sliding effect is called 'glissando', and composers ask for it when they want an amusing or a deliberately vulgar sound.

Horn

Range:

The modern *horn* has been developed from the seventeenth and eighteenth-century hunting horn. It is a conical tube about 3.6m long, coiled into a circular shape. The tube widens quite considerably towards the bell at one end, and the player puts his lips against a funnel-shaped mouthpiece. Like the trumpet, the horn has valves which change the overall length of the instrument at the touch of a finger. Because of the way it is coiled, the player supports the horn with his right hand resting in the bell. He can move his hand into the bell to adjust the tuning of the instrument, and for other effects as we shall see later.

Because the horn has a long tube, very narrow for most of its length, the higher notes of the harmonic series are more readily available. These high notes lie very close together, and it needs very delicate adjustment of the tension of the player's lips for him to be able to pick out the right one. The horn uses more of these high natural notes than any other brass instruments: that is why the horn is generally considered the most difficult brass instrument to play well.

Before the valves were invented, the player was restricted to the notes obtainable from one length of tube. In Bach's day, some horn players could play the extremely high natural notes, but after the middle of the eighteenth century composers stopped asking for them, and players used the middle of the range (up to the sixteenth note in the harmonic series). This meant that there were some gaps and some out-of-tune notes (see page 44). The player got round this by pushing his right hand into the bell and 'stopping' the notes – changing the natural open note by a semitone. But these stopped notes had a different quality. With the modern valve horn the player does not have to get extra notes with his hand, but he still 'stops' the horn for special effects.

Natural horns, like trumpets, had extra metal tubes called 'crooks' which the player could fit into his instrument to change the length and he often had a set of nine different ones.

The modern orchestral horn is usually a double instrument, a

The Brass

Horn

combination of two horns in one, enabling the player to switch immediately from a horn built on the fundamental note F, to one built a fourth higher, on B flat. The player uses three valves in the normal way for whichever 'side' of the horn is in operation.

Occasionally the principal horn player uses a single horn pitched in B flat.

The player is sometimes asked to put a mute in his instrument. He can also get a muted sound by putting his hand in the bell, which makes the horn sound distant. By pushing his hand well into the bell and blowing hard, he can produce a particularly brassy sound. In fact this sound is called *cuivré,* the French for brassy.

This was written for natural ('valveless') horns. The cross note in bar 7 would have been obtained by hand-stopping.

Normally the horn has a smooth, mellow tone quality, which makes it blend well in the orchestra, and bridges the gap between the brass and the woodwind family. Indeed, in orchestral music, it is sometimes difficult to tell the difference between the sound of the horn and the sound of the bassoon.

Tuba

Range:

The *bass tuba* provides the lowest notes in the brass family. Because of its wide conical bore, the tuba can produce its lowest natural note (the fundamental) with ease, and it fills in the big gap between the first and second natural notes (see the harmonic series on page 44) with the aid of the valves.

The orchestral bass tuba is only one of a whole family of tubas, They are comparatively modern instruments, first appearing in the 1820s.

Wagner made great use of a range of tuba-type instruments. Apart from the bass tuba, the tenor tuba is often used in the orchestra. This instrument is known in brass and military bands as the *euphonium,* and several famous tuba solos, including *Bydlo* from Ravel's orchestration of 'Pictures from an Exhibition', are usually played on a tenor instrument.

Like modern trombones and horns, tubas are usually built as 'double' instruments.

E♭ bass tuba

The Brass

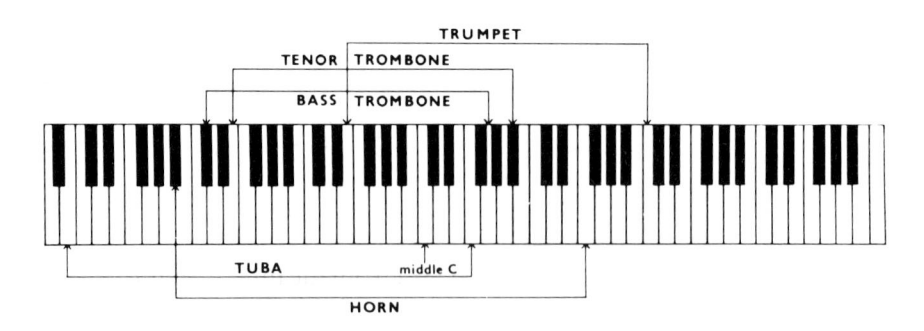

The range of orchestral brass instruments
(Top notes and bottom notes are in some cases approximate)

Saxophone

The *saxophone* comes in several varieties, according to its size. The common ones today are the *soprano, alto, tenor,* and *baritone*. There are also the *sopranino,* which is higher than the soprano saxophone, the *bass,* and very rarely, the *contrabass.*

The instruments of the saxophone family were invented in the 1840s by Adolphe Sax. The player produces vibrations with a single reed (as in the clarinet). But the tube is conical (not like the clarinet) and it is made of brass. The instrument is fingered much like a clarinet, but it overblows at the octave, like an oboe. The saxophone is used in military bands and in dance bands. It is not often used in the orchestra.

5 Percussion

Percussion instruments are those that are banged, tapped, or shaken. There are two main kinds of percussion instruments: those that can play definite notes; and those that have no definite notes, but can be played rhythmically or add a splash of colour.

Timpani

The *timpani* (or kettledrums) are the most important percussion instruments; together with the trumpets a pair of timpani was brought into the orchestra from the military parade ground during the seventeenth century. Originally, in the army, the timpani were smaller, slung on either side of a horse, and played by a mounted bandsman.

The drum consisted of a skin stretched over a deep copper bowl. When the skin was struck by a drum-stick it produced a note of definite pitch. For many years, the pitch of the drum could be changed by altering the tension of the skin (known as the 'drumhead' or simply 'head') by a series of hand screws positioned round the circumference of the drum.

Today, the head (either calf-skin or a synthetic plastic material) is tightened or slackened by a mechanism operated by a foot pedal. There are usually three or four timpani in a modern orchestra, each drum of a different size, and each tuned to a different note. The player can change the pitch of a drum at will. He is often asked to change the pitch of a drum during the music. This tuning must be inaudible to everyone but himself; thus the player is often to be seen operating the pedal and putting his ear close to the drumhead as he tests the pitch by flicking it with his finger or striking it gently with the drum-stick. The timpanist has a variety of sticks to choose from, ranging from soft spongy ones to hard wooden ones – all producing a different tone quality.

He can play a 'roll', striking the drumhead alternately with his two sticks very rapidly. Or he can play quite separate notes, in single strokes.

Composers often ask for a sliding effect ('glissando') where the timpanist continues to play a roll as he changes the pitch of the note with the pedal.

Percussion

Bass drum

The *bass drum,* with the triangle and cymbals, came to the orchestra from the Turkish-style military bands that became popular in Europe during the eighteenth century. The bass drum is a large drum that stands on its side. It can have two drumheads (two surfaces of stretched skin) or only one, when it is sometimes called the 'gong drum'. It is often found in British orchestras with one drumhead and it looks like a giant tambourine, without the jingles.

    A bass drum can be played with single taps or by using two sticks (like large padded timpani sticks) the player can perform a roll. A soft roll sounds like distant thunder. Unlike the timpani, the bass drum produces sounds of an indefinite pitch.

Side drum

The *side drum* (or snare drum) is another instrument that came to the orchestra from the army. In the army it is carried slung to the side of the player. In the orchestra it is supported on a stand. It has two drumheads, and the player strikes the upper one. The lower head has strings of gut or springy metal stretched across it. These are called snares. When the player hits the top surface, each blow pushes the skin, which pushes the air inside the drum against the bottom skin. This bottom skin in turn pushes against the snares and the result is a dry, rattling noise. The player uses hard wooden sticks, and by giving two taps with each stick alternately to the rhythm of 'Mummy, Daddy: Mummy, Daddy' said very quickly without a pause, he can produce a very quick roll.

Cymbals

Cymbals are two thin plates of brass. The player can clash them together very loudly. He can make them sweep past each other with a violent swish. Or he can gently brush one with the other. He can hold up one cymbal and hit it with a soft stick. Or he can mount it on a stand and play a roll with two sticks, producing a wonderful shimmering sound.

Triangle

The *triangle* is a metal rod in the shape of a triangle, with one corner

Percussion

Percussion (glockenspiel, xylophone, tom-tom, cymbal, bass drum, timpani)

open. By quickly moving the beater up and down in one corner of the triangle, the player can produce a roll.

Gong

The *gong* came to the orchestra from the Far East. It is a large disc of metal, usually with the edge bent over. The player can play it with single strokes, or he can play a roll on it.

Tamtam

The *tamtam* is usually taken to be another name for the gong. Some composers make a distinction between the two instruments. The tamtam is often a bigger disc of metal without the edges turned over. In sound, the gong can be said to produce a 'bong' and the tamtam a 'crash'.

Tambourine

The *tambourine* is like a very small drum, with only one drumhead. Round the side there are small metal discs that jingle against each other when the drumhead is struck. You can shake the tambourine; hit it with your hand; bang it against your knee. Sometimes the player is asked to moisten his thumb, and rub it round the edge of the instrument. This makes a sound like a tinkling 'raspberry'.

There are many other percussion instruments that are sometimes used in the orchestra:

Castanets

Castanets are two hollowed-out pieces of hard wood which are clicked together. They are often used to give music a Spanish flavour. In Spain the two pieces are linked together and the player holds both sections of the instrument in one hand, the fingers tapping one part against the other, which is supported by the thumb. In the orchestra, the castanets are usually mounted on a stick.

Whip

The *whip* is two flat pieces of wood that are hinged together. When struck together, they produce a noise like the crack of a whip.

Chinese wood block	The *Chinese wood block* is a partly hollow block of wood that gives a penetrating 'tock' when struck.
	These Latin American instruments have come to the orchestra from the dance band:
Maracas	*Maracas* are South American instruments which look and sound like a pair of baby's rattles.
Claves	*Claves* are two wooden sticks that are clicked together.
Bongo drums	*Bongo drums* are rather like miniature timpani; they are played with the hands.

Apart from the timpani (and to some extent the bongo drums) all the percussion instruments so far mentioned produce notes of an indefinite pitch.

By taking three timpani and tuning them to *soh, doh,* and *me,* you can give a splendid performance of 'Come to the Cookhouse Door'. It would be impossible to do that with three side drums, or three bass drums.

All the following percussion instruments are able to play tunes:

Celeste — The *celeste* looks like a miniature piano. It has black and white keys, and the player at the keyboard plays it in the same way as you would a piano. The keys operate hammers which strike metal plates. The sound is silvery and delicate.

Xylophone — The *xylophone* is made of strips of hard wood each tuned to a note. The strips are laid out like the notes on a piano keyboard, the 'white' notes in front, and 'black' notes behind. The player hits the strips of wood with wooden beaters, or sometimes, for soft effects, with hard rubber ones. The xylophone produces a bright, dry, hard sound.

Glockenspiel The *glockenspiel* is made in the same way as the xylophone except that the bars are made of metal and not wood. It sounds rather like the celeste but with a 'harder' tone.

Tubular bells The *tubular bells* are metal tubes that are hung in a frame. These tubes produce sounds like church bells. The player hits the top of the tube with a wooden mallet.

Vibraphone The *vibraphone* is like a large-sized glockenspiel. There are two rows of tuned metal bars, but under each bar there is a tube, which acts as a resonator to the bar. In each of the tubes is a small fan driven by electricity. When the player hits the bar, the resonator picks up the sound and the fan gives it a throbbing effect.

6 How the Orchestra Grew

Strings and harpsichord

The modern orchestra has grown up round the string family. During the latter part of the seventeenth century we read of the 'King's 24 violins' at the French Court. This string group set a fashion that spread to England and to the rest of Europe. At first there was no regular method of dividing up the strings; but by 1700 the basic pattern of the string orchestra was set:
first violins, second violins, violas, and cellos, with the double basses playing the same part as the cellos an octave lower.

This grouping of the strings has lasted down to the present day, except that during the last 150 years the cellos have been allowed to leave the bass part occasionally and use their expressive tenor voices much more.

The early string orchestra was always grouped round a keyboard instrument, usually a *harpsichord*. The harpsichord looks rather like a grand piano, but instead of the strings being hit with hammers, as in the piano, the strings in the harpsichord are plucked by small quills. The 'twanging' sound of the harpsichord had 'bite' to it, which could be felt clearly by the groups of string players round it. The harpsichord player gave the lead to the group and filled out the harmonies of the music. It could also play the part of any instrument that might not be available.

Other instruments played with the strings and harpsichord. Between about 1680 and 1750 there were no hard and fast rules about which instruments they should be. Oboes and bassoons often did, and so did the trumpets and horns. Composers wrote music for the instruments that happened to be at hand, and they were not fussy if a flute played an oboe part, or the other way round.

When Bach (1685–1750) was working for Prince Leopold of Cöthen he had a small band of eighteen musicians, of which the harpsichord and the strings were the main section. Besides the strings, Bach had other instruments at his disposal. If a piece were made up of several movements, he would often add different wind instruments to each movement for a change of colour.

The growth of the orchestra

Time	Where it played	Conductor	Instruments	Average no. of players
up to 1700	Mainly in churches and theatres; 'Concerts' usually given in private houses of noblemen	Directed from the keyboard	*Always:* violins, violas, cellos double basses keyboard instrument (usually harpsichord) *and very often:* oboes or flutes bassoons trumpets, drums	20
1700 to 1750	Churches, theatres (Operas); private houses of noblemen; music in public gardens	Directed from keyboard or violin desk	strings as before harpsichord oboes and/or flutes bassoons horns trumpets, drums	20–40
1750 to 1800	Public concerts; private houses of noblemen; opera houses; theatres	Directed from keyboard or violin desk	strings as before 2 flutes, 2 oboes 2 clarinets, 2 bassoons 2 horns, 2 trumpets drums	30–50

Classical orchestra

Up to the end of the eighteenth century, a composer was usually a musical servant in an aristocratic household; and he was expected to provide musical entertainment when it was needed. During the eighteenth century, at a princely court, the composer would have an orchestra of anything from twenty to sixty players at his disposal, in which he would play the harpsichord or sometimes the violin, conducting at the same time. One of the chief jobs for him and his orchestra would be to accompany singers; for until about 1760 people generally preferred to listen to vocal music. Another job the orchestra had to do was to provide pleasant background music for dinner parties and receptions. In these circumstances people would not pay much

Time	Where it played	Conductor	Instruments	Average no. of players
1800 to 1850	Public concerts; opera houses; theatres	Conducted with stick	strings as before 2 flutes, 2 oboes 2 clarinets 2 bassoons *and very often:* piccolo, cor anglais bass clarinet double bassoon 4 horns 3 trumpets 3 trombones 1 tuba percussion	60–80
1850 to 1900	Public concerts; opera houses	Conducted with stick	strings as before woodwind as before brass as before but horns and trumpets with valves, much extra percussion	80–100

attention to the orchestra itself and the composer would not be very particular about which instruments played as long as there was a reasonable sound. During the course of the eighteenth century, however, a new kind of music called the symphony was developing, which was played by the orchestra on its own. People listened to this music for its own sake and, as the orchestra became the centre of attention, composers began to take a great deal of trouble over the way the orchestra was made up. The strings and harpsichord were still the backbone of the orchestra, and oboes and bassoons had become permanent fixtures. Flutes played in the woodwind section, sometimes instead of the oboes, and later on, with the oboes. Towards the end of the century, clarinets became more and more popular. By about 1750 practically every orchestra had a pair of horns, whose smooth and mellow tone made a bridge between the high and low instruments, and also added strength to the wind section. Courtly households usually had trumpets and drums, and although these were not necessarily part of the orchestra, they were often called in for special effects.

The court of Mannheim in Germany had a very famous orchestra, and Mozart, who heard it in 1777, wrote: 'The orchestra is excellent and strong. On either side there are ten or eleven violins, four violas, two oboes, two flutes and two clarinets, two horns, four cellos, four bassoons and four double basses, also trumpets and drums.'

The greatest composers of orchestral music in the eighteenth century were Mozart and Haydn, and towards the end of the century, when they both wrote their most famous symphonies, the usual sort of orchestra would be made up of strings; two each of flutes, oboes, clarinets, bassoons, horns, and trumpets; and drums. The harpsichord and the piano still played in orchestral music, but they were becoming unnecessary. When Haydn visited London in 1793 he conducted his symphonies from the piano.

Beethoven

Beethoven (1770–1827) found that the orchestra that Haydn and Mozart had used was not always powerful enough for his strong, dramatic music. He also wanted more variety of tone colour. For these reasons, he brought the trombones into the orchestra (the trombones had played in operatic and church music before, but not in a symphony). He added the piccolo and a double bassoon to the woodwind section; he increased the horns to three or four; he gave the timpani a more important part to play. Beethoven wanted a larger force of strings too, and often made the violins play higher than they had before.

Berlioz and Wagner

The music of the French composer Berlioz (1803–69) is wonderfully written for orchestra. Berlioz drew sounds from instruments which previous composers had never thought of. He wrote a book on *orchestration* (writing for orchestra) which is still studied by young composers. Berlioz sometimes wanted the strings to play 'col legno', and sometimes asked for wind instruments to be played with mutes, and for special 'stopped' effects from the horns. He suggested new ways of playing percussion instruments (like hitting a cymbal with a timpani stick). Berlioz dreamed of an ideal orchestra made up of 240 strings, 30 pianos, 30 harps, with matching numbers of wind and percussion instruments!

By about 1850 big improvements had been made in the brass instruments of the orchestra. Horns and trumpets were being made with valves, which meant that they could play any note in their range. The German composer Wagner (1813–83) took advantage of these improvements in brass instruments, and wrote magnificent music for them. In his four music dramas which form *The Ring,* he uses eight horns as well as trombones, trumpets, and tubas. Woodwind instruments were also being improved during the nineteenth century so that they became easier to play, more 'in tune', and more expressive. The bass clarinet was invented, and Wagner added that to his woodwind instruments in *The Ring*. In fact, *The Ring* called for fifteen woodwind, twenty-one brass, harps, and percussion, sixteen first violins, sixteen second, twelve violas, twelve cellos and eight double basses – over one hundred instruments in all. (Compare this with Bach's orchestra of eighteen or Haydn's of about forty players.)

Conductors

Conductors as we know them, conducting with a stick (or baton) and standing on a little platform in front of the orchestra, have only been in existence for just over a hundred years. In the eighteenth century orchestras were directed from the keyboard. (In churches, however, and other large places where the musicians would be spread about, a gentleman would just beat time with a long staff or a roll of paper.)

By the nineteenth century, the keyboard instrument had become unnecessary. But orchestras were growing larger, and music was being written with more expression and changes of speed in it. At first, the leader (the chief violinist) waved his bow occasionally to give the players a lead, but soon, from about 1820 onwards, a musician who was not playing an instrument as well took over controlling the orchestra with a stick.

The orchestra today

At the end of the last century and the beginning of this, many composers were writing for enormous orchestras. It is not surprising that during this century some composers have gone to the opposite extreme and experimented with much smaller combinations of instruments.

Modern composers have invented a whole new world of sound through treating traditional instruments electronically. A contact microphone attached directly to an instrument or a normal (air) microphone can feed input into a ring modulator, controlled by another performer, who modifies and transforms the sound to be heard through the loudspeakers. Players themselves can treat the sound of their own instruments through electronic filter devices controlled by foot pedals, which filter out harmonics and change the quality and sometimes the apparent pitch of a sound. There are also various kinds of tape delay systems which allow the player to manipulate infinite echo effects. These new sounds can be heard in both 'serious' music and rock.

The tape recorder has become another instrument of the orchestra. A tape of sound material (usually prepared by the composer) is played as part of the performance of an orchestral work, as directed in the score. The audience hears the instruments of the orchestra and, through loudspeakers, the pre-recorded sounds of the tape. Live and electronic sounds are thus combined in varying textures.

The usual size of a symphony orchestra is between about 80 and 100 players. Additional instruments that are often used in modern music

How the Orchestra Grew

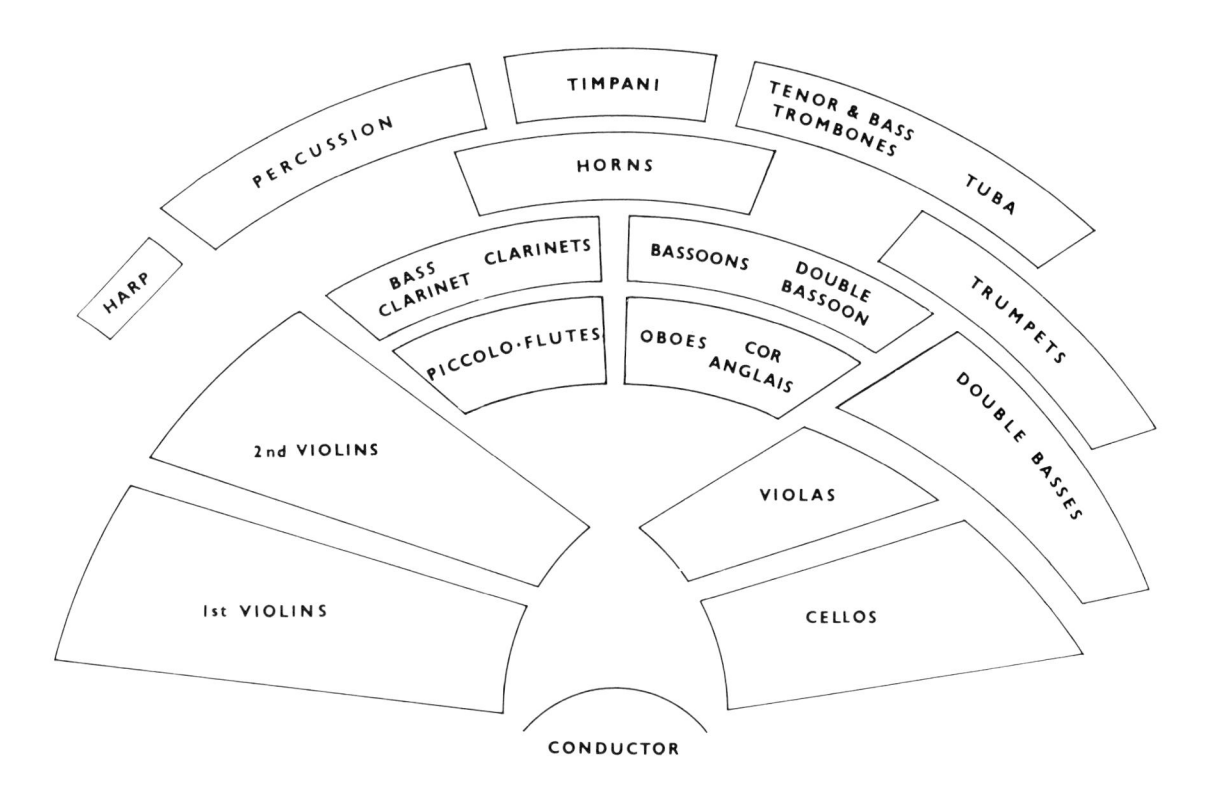

This is how you often see the players in an orchestra. Sometimes you will see the trumpets and trombones on the other side, where the percussion is marked here. Sometimes the horns are slightly more to the left. Some conductors put the second violins on their right (where the cellos are shown here), and the cellos more in the centre of the string group.

are brought in as 'extras'. That is to say, they are only brought in when they are needed. Modern composers often use a great many percussion instruments, and the piano is also frequently used as a member of the percussion department. Since the harpsichord was dropped out of the orchestra, the only plucked sounds have been those of the harp and pizzicato strings. Composers nowadays are taking a new interest in plucked sounds, and they sometimes ask for a mandolin or a guitar in the orchestra.

Conductors usually vary the size of the orchestra to suit the style of the music they are playing. They can build up, or, when they are playing eighteenth-century music, cut down the strength of the orchestra according to the music they are performing.

Nowadays you can hear small orchestras of strings and harpsichord, with one or two additional wind instruments, that specialize in playing eighteenth-century music. Also today there are ensembles which perform medieval and renaissance music on authentic reconstructions of old instruments. In these ensembles we can recognize many forerunners of the instruments described in this book. But for the most part these instruments are outside the scope of this guide.